Positive Praise!

"James, you are *Chicken Soup* for so many souls, including mine. Keep sharing your heart and your wisdom."

-Jack Canfield
Co-author, #1 New York Times Best-Selling book series
Chicken Soup for the Soul

"James, thanks for all of your support and for sharing your story with us. You're such a good person. Love and blessings!"

-Kimberly Kirberger
Co-author, *Chicken Soup for the Teenage Soul*

"James Malinchak will motivate and inspire you to exceed your potential. *Teenagers Tips for Success* should be read by all students!"

-Rudy Ruettiger
the man who inspired the Tri-Star blockbuster movie *"RUDY"*

"James Malinchak empowers teenagers to reach their dreams!"

-Joe Paterno
Head Football Coach, Penn State University

"As a professional athlete, I understand how important it is for teenagers to have positive role models. Jim Malinchak is not only an excellent role model, but his book provides teens with much needed guidance."

-Loy Vaught
NBA Player, Detroit Pistons

"We run basketball camps for teenagers nationwide and we're going to give every camper a copy of *Teenagers Tips for Success!* We're also going to arrange for James to speak at every camp. He is absolutely the best speaker for teenagers we have ever heard!"

-Jennifer Tower, CFO
Play Like A Pro, Inc. and Summer Camp Coordinator

"James, you are very impressive. We have about 30,000 students in our school district and you're someone we would like to bring in to talk to all of our young people."

-Ken Biermann
Director of Student Support Services
Glendale Unified School District (Glendale, CA)

"Your book will be used in our Guidance Office for use with our students. The area of the book in which I am most impressed is the practical application suggestions for students."

-Randall E. Marino, Principal
Monessen High School (Monessen, PA)

"Teenagers are the world's greatest resource. This book provides them with practical, easy-to-understand principles for creating success. A *must* read for every young person."

-Cathy Switzer
Coordinator, Library Media Services
Kaukauna Area Schools (Green Bay, WI)

"James, your book is one that should be read and re-read. It is a road map to success. But beyond that, meeting you personally, I know that you are committed to making a difference!"

-Kiki Vandeweghe
former NBA Player
Chairman of the Board, Sports Group International, Inc.

Touching the Lives of Teenagers Worldwide...

"Thank you very much for answering my request for more information for my book report!"

-**Yael Daniel, age 14**
(Kibbutz, Israel)

"Your book taught me that you have to believe in yourself and never give up, even if you fail trying to accomplish something. I just wanted to say thanks for the book. It's really cool!"

-**Mike Seibel, age 12**
(Appleton, WI)

"I loved your story in *Chicken Soup for the Teenage Soul*. It made me think about others!"

-**Maria Catalina, age 16**
(Rio Pierdras, Puerto Rico)

"The lecture brought to my attention that now is when I need to start planning my life.....one of the *best lectures* I have heard that relates to my life."

-**Michael Dyblnis, age 16**
(Los Angeles, CA)

"You are by far the BEST speaker I have ever heard!"

-**Joey Hurzel, sophomore**
Carson High School (Carson City, NV)

"You are for sure the BEST speaker we have ever had in our school!"

-**Sarah Tuff**
Miller High School
(Regina-Saskatchewan, Canada)

Published by
POSITIVE PUBLISHING
P.O. Box 32
Monessen, PA 15062

Printed in the United States of America

Library of Congress Catalog Card Number: 96-092489

ISBN 0-9646924-1-4

Text Editing by Gay Simmons and Joe Woodward
Cover Graphics by Lin Alvarez

Warning - Disclaimer
The purpose of this book is to educate and entertain. The author or publisher does not guarantee that anyone following the ideas, tips, suggestions, techniques or strategies will become successful. The author and publisher shall have neither liability or responsibility to anyone with respect to any loss or damage caused, or alleged to be caused, directly or indirectly by the information contained in this book.

Teenagers

Tips for

SUCCESS!

**Create a Future,
Achieve Your Dreams
and Become *Very* Successful**

James Malinchak

Dedication

With love I dedicate this book to my mother Betty and my father Walter, who taught me many lessons in life. Your love, guidance, and support have made me the person I am today. Thank you for all that you have done for me. I *really* appreciate it!

A Special Thank You

People rarely accomplish anything without the help of others. I really appreciate some special people who have helped, guided, and supported me in the pursuit of my dreams. I would not be where I am today without their help.

My sincere appreciation to: my parents and family, (Wally, Cindy and Vicki) for helping me create and shape my future; William Malinchak for your advice and encouragement; Melanie DuBois for your love and support; Nate Bailey for your advice, but more importantly, your friendship, Gary Steiner for your help and guidance, and to everyone who has helped with this book and my speaking career.

Contents

Author's Note: Why this Book is Needed!

I love talking to teenagers. They're never afraid to tell you what they're going to accomplish in their lives. The more teenagers I talk to the more I realize that, although they dream of becoming successful, there's a problem. They're never taught the essential principles for achieving success.

Society tells teenagers if they go to school they will become successful. School is a very important part of success, but there's more to it than that. A school education is only one part of creating success.

The other part of creating success is a *Real World* education. Skills such as goal setting, making contacts, communicating with others, choosing a career, managing money, overcoming obstacles and making choices. Teenagers need to learn these principles in order to create a successful future.

This book will provide teenagers with a road map to success! More importantly, it teaches teenagers the essential priciples for succeeding in the *Real World.* Success does not begin when we graduate from college or land our first "big" job. Success starts during our teenage years. This is the time when we can put these key principles in motion and begin to create and shape our future.

This book is simple, short and to the point. *Teenagers Tips for Success!* will not take long to read but it can be life changing. It contains some of the most valuable information teenagers will ever learn. This is information that should be taught in <u>every</u> school.

The principles in this book have one objective:

To Make Teenagers Successful!

It All Starts with a Dream

"I visualized where I wanted to be, what kind of player I wanted to become. I knew exactly where I wanted to go, and I focused on getting there."

-Michael Jordan

Since the age of 13, I dreamed about playing big-time, NCAA Division 1 college basketball. Often I found myself on the playground dribbling through my legs and around my back pretending that I was playing for the North Carolina Tarheels. Other times, I would be shooting long jump shots helping the Kentucky Wildcats beat the Indiana Hoosiers for the National Championship. And of course, I was named the game MVP.

Even when I played for my junior high school team, I would often dream during practice and games. I pictured a standing-room-only crowd, bands playing loudly, fans screaming at the top of their lungs, cheerleaders being flipped high into the air, TV cameras filming and broadcasting nationwide on ESPN, and of course, the energetic Dick Vitale exciting TV viewers with his enthusiastic play-by-play commentary.

Basketball always seemed more exciting when I juiced it up with these visions. As I look back, I realize that I daydreamed about basketball in that way because my dreams were a vision of the future I desired. It's good to daydream. Dreaming allows us to visualize what we desire most. It allows us to form a mental picture of the success of realizing our dream. The problem with dreaming is that most people think their dreams will never come true.

I was one of those people, until my junior year in high school. A teacher, who I respected highly, made a comment that changed my attitude. Mrs. Monaghan said, "You can do anything you put your mind to. *If You Can Dream It, You Can Do It!*"

From that moment, I never settled for anything less than my dreams. If I dreamed about achieving something, I pursued it until I had achieved it. Anything that I have ever accomplished in my life began with dreaming about it first.

Dreaming, and believing that you will achieve your dream, is half the battle. Once you are determined to achieve your dream nothing will stop you.

> *"All our dreams can come true - if we have the courage to pursue them."*
> **-Walt Disney**

As I advanced to the high school basketball level, my dream of playing big-time college basketball grew stronger. I still envisioned playing on television and in sold out arenas. Only this time it would be different. I would not stop with only a dream. I would turn it into a reality. As Mrs. Monaghan said, "if you can dream it, you can do it." I was beginning to believe her.

I turned my dream into a goal, which is the first step to realizing your dream. My goal was to land a Division 1 basketball scholarship. But as others became aware of my goal, many laughed and said it couldn't be done. I heard all of the reasons why I would fail.....not quick enough, not fast enough, doesn't shoot well enough, doesn't have the athletic ability, plays at a small high school, comes from a small town, no one else has ever done it, so how could he? What those people didn't know was that I had a dream and nothing would stop me from realizing it.

My dream was beginning to turn into a reality during my senior year of high school. College coaches from around the country were becoming interested in me. My mailbox was filled with letters from many schools: Duke, Arizona, DePaul, Auburn, Georgia, Miami (FL), Hawaii, South Carolina, East Carolina, Maryland, Florida State, and yes, even North Carolina.

My dream came true when I accepted a full scholarship to play basketball at the University of Cincinnati. The first time I stepped on the court for a game against the University of Louisville I knew I had made it. Louisville was the #3 ranked team in the nation and we were playing at their legendary arena, Freedom Hall. It was just as I had dreamed it would be.

There was a standing-room-only crowd of 19,000 people. The Louisville band was jamming. Fans were screaming. Cheerleaders were being tossed high into the air. Television cameras were everywhere, and my man Dick Vitale was there getting the TV viewers fired up.

As I stood next to some of the great Louisville players such as "Never-A-Nervous" Pervis Ellison and Felton Spencer (both are now in the NBA), I realized that I had done it! My dream of making it to the top level of college basketball was fulfilled. Mrs. Monaghan was right,

"IF YOU CAN DREAM IT, YOU CAN DO IT!"

This simple phrase is something you need to remember for the rest of your life. Dreams are not difficult to fulfill. We only think they are because most people are afraid to pursue their dreams. Be different. You have the ability to achieve anything that you desire. Simply, make the decision to turn your dream into a goal. Then pursue your goal until it is realized.

> *"Cherish your visions and your dreams as they are the blue prints of your ultimate achievements."*
> **-Napoleon Hill**

Success starts with a dream. Anything that you wish to accomplish in life must first be pictured in your mind, felt in your heart, and desired in your soul. Things are not achieved by chance. Sure, there are times when luck plays a little part. But to set out and accomplish something, you first must form a mental picture of how you would feel and what positive things will happen when your dream is realized.

All successful people dream, even some of the most popular people in the world.

At seventeen, *Mariah Carey* was a waitress and wore sneakers with holes while pursuing her musical dream. Today, she has sold over 16 million albums, had her first five singles hit #1 and won two Grammy awards.

Bill Clinton didn't become the leader of our country because he was looking for a new job. He had a dream of becoming the President of the United States. He believed in his dream and set out to achieve it. In November 1992, Bill Clinton was elected the President of the United States.

> *"Imagination turns possibilities into reality."*
>
> **-Unknown**

Nothing great has ever been achieved without first dreaming about it. Dreaming allows us to picture what we desire most. The problem with dreaming is that most young people believe that their dreams can never be real. Or, they listen to those who tell them that they'll never achieve their dreams.

As you begin trying to accomplish certain goals in your life, you will meet people who will criticize you and try to bring you down. Stay away from these negative people. You don't need negative thinking people in your life.

Don't worry about what others think. It only matters what you think. Don't try to please others. You only have to please yourself.

If your friends do not support and encourage you then they are not your true friends. True friends will believe in you and will help you figure out how to achieve your dreams.

Those who tell you that it can't be done are the very people who are scared to pursue their own dreams. They are jealous of anyone who succeeds because if you are moving forward and achieving goals in your life, then people will notice you and not notice them.

> *"Those who say it cannot be done, should not interrupt those doing it."*
>
> **-Unknown**

The type of people you associate with reflects the type of person you will become. If you associate with negative people, then you will eventually become a negative person. If you hang around positive people who have dreams and goals, then you will develop successful, winning characteristics.

You need to study success. Find someone who has the kind of happiness and success that you would like to have in your life, then copy them. Learn what they have done, then try to follow their path because *Success Leaves Clues!*

When you finish reading this book, take five minutes to think about those qualities you admire in other people. Which of those qualities would you like to have? Write down these ideas, memorize them, and begin practicing them everyday. Soon, those qualities will become a habit and they will become the qualities that you have yourself.

Failure Is Good

> *"Failure is good. It's fertilizer. Everything I've learned about coaching I've learned from making mistakes."*
>
> **-Rick Pitino**
> **head basketball coach, Univ. of Kentucky**
> **1996 NCAA National Champions**

There's a chance that you may fail while trying to achieve your dreams. You must understand this. No one said success would be easy. The important thing is that you never quit or give up when you fail.

Successful people are not afraid to fail. Failure is a good teacher. Learn what you did wrong or what you have to do better to succeed. Failure is a part of trying. I would rather fail trying to accomplish something than not even try at all. Don't quit when faced with failure, you may be closer to succeeding than you think.

Thomas Edison failed approximately 2,000 times before finally inventing the light bulb. Rather than getting discouraged and quitting when he had an unsuccessful attempt, he would simply say that he was one step closer to finding the correct procedure.

Abraham Lincoln lost approximately eight elections before becoming President of the United States. Although he continued to lose elections, he never quit pursuing his dreams.

Great accomplishments rarely occur on the first try. You will fail. It's just a part of life. The way to overcome failure is to, first, realize that it happens, then learn from it. Failure will teach you valuable lessons about succeeding.

> *"Persistence is the ability to face defeat again and again without giving up - to push on in the face of great difficulty, knowing that victory can be yours."*
>
> **-Unknown**

> *"You don't learn, evolve, become more of a human being by winning Oscars, making money, and living in Malibu. You learn by disappointments."*
>
> **-Jodie Foster, Actress**

Turn Your Dreams into Goals

> *"If you don't know where you are going how can you expect to get there?"*
>
> -Basil S. Walsh

Webster's New World Dictionary defines a goal as, "an end that one strives to attain." In other words, a goal is something that you desire (a dream) and, therefore, set out to achieve.

The purpose of goals is to focus your attention. You will not progress until your goals are clearly defined. When you can form a clear picture of exactly what it is that you want to achieve and how satisfied you would feel after achieving it, you will develop a desire. This desire will ignite a fire inside of you that pushes you toward success. Once this desire is felt, your determination to succeed becomes more powerful than any feeling of giving up.

Not having goals is like trying to drive a car without a road map to a state you have never visited. How can you expect to reach your destination without proper direction? The same is true of anything you wish to accomplish in your life. You need a plan, a road map.

NBA Player *Loy Vaught* played at the University of Michigan. He led his school to the NCAA National Championship in 1989 and was the #13 overall selection in the 1990 NBA draft by the Los Angeles Clippers. He consistently averages double figures in points and rebounds and is considered one of the premier power forwards in the game. Loy works as hard as anyone to achieve his goals. I know this because during the NBA off season, we work out together in the weight room.

I asked Loy what makes him successful in life and basketball. Loy says, "I always have a vision of where I want to go and I set goals that relate to my vision. I realistically create a vision of how I want my future to be and I write down my goals."

Loy also wanted to offer what he feels are some key points to achieving success. Loy says, "I'm a big believer in discipline and doing certain things that may be unpleasant in order to achieve a long term goal. Weight lifting in the summer or working on my basketball weaknesses are sometimes unpleasant and difficult, but I understand that these are a few sacrifices I must make if I want to achieve my goals. The best in life doesn't come easy. Even when I hit difficult times or obstacles, I stay focused on my goals."

> *"You've got to be very careful if you don't know where you are going, because you might not get there."*
>
> -Yogi Berra

It Works!

My senior basketball season was my first experience with goal setting. I decided to test the theory that if you write down your goals, somehow you accomplish them.

The day before our first practice, I sat alone in the locker room with a pencil and sheet of paper. I began listing all of the goals that I wanted to achieve by the end of the season. Some of them were set very high. Listed are the 20 goals I set for my senior year.

Goals I will accomplish this season!

1) Average over 20 points per game
2) Average over 7 assists per game
3) Average over 5 rebounds per game
4) Shoot 85% from the free throw line
5) Shoot 60% form the field
6) Shoot 50% from 3-point range
7) Win the section title
8) Win the Western Pennsylvania Interscholastic Athletic League (WPIAL) championship
9) Win the state championship
10) Be selected to play in the Dapper Dan Roundball All-American Game (A game for the top high school players in the country)
11) Make first team All-Section
12) Make first team All-WPIAL

13) Make first team All-State
14) Be named All-American
15) Average 20 points in the Las Vegas Holiday Christmas Tournament
16) Win section MVP
17) Win WPIAL MVP
18) Win State MVP
19) Be recruited by major Division 1 colleges
20) Accept a full scholarship to a major NCAA Division 1 college that plays many televised games

At the end of the season, I looked at the list. I figured I probably had accomplished a few that I had written down. To my surprise, I found that I had accomplished 18 of the 20 goals listed. The two that I didn't achieve were barely missed. They were:

8) Win a WPIAL championship (We lost in the semi-finals)

14) Be named All-American (I was named Honorable Mention)

After my experience, I was convinced. If you write down your goals, somehow they come true. It's almost like magic!

Write Down Your Goals

> *"The indispensable first step to getting the things you want out of life is this: decide what you want."*
>
> **-Ben Stein**

So how do you set goals? The following exercise will help you. On the top of a sheet of paper write the following:

"Goals I Will Accomplish!"

1 Year   3 Years   5 Years

List the goals you WILL accomplish in the next year, the next three years and the next five years. Write down any and all of your dreams. It doesn't matter whether you believe that you can actually achieve them. The important thing is to write them down.

Write down as many as you desire. Don't be shy. This is your chance to dream big. Write down places you would like to visit, people you would like to meet, activities you would like to do, things you would like to achieve. Write down whatever you desire in your heart.

After making your list, write beside each goal the exact date you WILL accomplish it. This is an important part of goal setting because it places a deadline on your goal. You have now obligated yourself to achieve it by a certain date because you are creating a contract with yourself.

> *"Until input (thought) is linked to a goal (purpose) there can be no intelligent accomplishment."*
>
> **-Unknown**

What happens after making this contract with yourself is that your goals automatically become stored in your mind, just as you would store data in a computer. Now your list of goals becomes your checklist. The same as if you had listed items on a grocery checklist. A grocery checklist allows you to see and remember what you need to get at the store. A goal checklist allows you to see and remember what you desire to achieve in life.

Once your mind is programmed with the data of what you WILL accomplish, you begin moving toward achieving your goals. Before you realize it, you start to achieve your goals.

It's like magic when you write down your goals and place a deadline on achieving them. Somehow, you begin to achieve them.

At the end of your goal checklist, after you have written down ALL of your goals, it is very important for you to sign and date the paper. This commits you to pursuing them because it is now a formal contract with yourself. There can be no one to blame but yourself if you fail to pursue your goals.

Look at your goals routinely, once or twice a week. Keep showing and telling your mind that these are the things that you WILL accomplish in your life!

> *"The world has a habit of making room for the person whose words and actions show that they know where they are going."*
>
> **-Unknown**

Do You Have an Address Book?

> *"Meet people, then stay in touch FOREVER!*
> *You just never know where it could lead."*
>
> **-James Malinchak**

I had a childhood friend named Michael. When we were teenagers we would hang out together, playing basketball and football. As we entered high school, my goals led me toward pursuing a college basketball scholarship while Michael's led him toward pursuing a boxing career. Although we were not able to spend as much time together, we still remained friends.

After high school graduation, our paths headed in two separate directions. Michael moved to Detroit to train for a boxing career while I played college basketball at the University of Cincinnati and later at the University of Hawaii.

After graduating from college, I moved to Los Angeles to begin my career as a stockbroker. One day I picked up the morning newspaper and turned to the sports page. As I glanced over the page, I came across the following headline: *Evander Holyfield to defend World Heavyweight Boxing Title against Michael Moorer.* I couldn't believe it. My childhood friend was about to fight for the heavyweight title. I was so excited and thrilled that he had the opportunity to realize his dream.

I called a mutual friend of ours in our hometown to find out if he knew how to get in touch with Michael. He did. Michael was staying at Caesar's Palace Resort & Casino in Las Vegas.

I was able to get a message to Michael, leaving my phone number. I thought he might not remember our childhood friendship. But he did and returned my call. He said it was nice to hear from an old friend and was surprised by my call.

I promised Michael that I would be there for his big day. He told me to call him when I arrived so we could before the fight.

Michael defeated Evander Holyfield to become the World Heavyweight Boxing Champion and I was there to see it. All because of a simple contact and friendship that started when we were teenagers.

Communication Is The Key

If you were to ask me what is the single most important skill needed for anyone to become successful, without hesitation, I would reply communication. You communicate with people everyday in every area of your life. This includes school, sports, business, family situations, talking on the phone, talking to a group. How well you communicate will determine people's perception of you, meaning how people think of you as a person.

Developing good communication skills as a teenager can make you "super successful" for the rest of your life. One of the key ingredients of successful communication skills is making contacts. The contacts you make everyday will help you to succeed.

People are the shortcut to success in the *Real World.* The more people you know, the more opportunities you will have.

Forget about fancy computers, expensive cars or a big office. Nothing will be more important to your success than a simple $2.99 address book that can be purchased at any drug store. This is the secret to success. Every person you build a relationship with for the rest of your life must be listed in your book.

Get to know as many people as possible. You never know who is influential, or who knows whom. I'm a firm believer that, in today's society, who you know can help you get ahead faster than anything else.

Diversify your contacts by meeting different kinds of people. Take the initiative to introduce yourself, start a conversation, and build a rapport.

Equally as important as meeting people is staying in touch. Meeting a person once will not help you in the future. You need to build a relationship, get their address and phone number, list them in your address book, then stay in touch forever!

Send them thank-you notes, birthday cards, Christmas cards, Thanksgiving cards, anniversary cards, and basic letters. Call them periodically and occasionally get together for a quick visit.

You need to meet people, not only for business opportunities, but for personal interests as well. Take the initiative to introduce yourself to people, start a conversation, build a rapport, become friends, get their addresses and phone numbers, list them in your address book, then, most importantly, stay in touch. You never know where it may lead.

The process I just described works. If you're skeptical, here's proof.

About two years ago I was in a buffet line at a dinner party, and I noticed that **Dennis Hopper,** famous actor in *Speed, Waterworld* and the NIKE shoe commercials for the NFL, was also in line. He left the buffet line and sat at a table that had an open seat right next to him. This was my big chance to test my networking skills.

After taking a deep breath I walked over to Dennis and asked him if the seat next to him was taken. It wasn't, so I sat down and began eating. I was a little nervous about introducing myself. After all why would a successful person like Dennis Hopper want to talk with a young 24-year-old "kid?"

But this was my big chance and I wasn't about to blow it. I took another deep breath and took the initiative to introduced myself. To my surprise, Dennis smiled, shook my hand and started a conversation. For the next hour, we talked about everything from sports to travel to movies.

As Dennis was leaving, I asked him for his address and phone number. To my surprise, he was happy to give it to me. He is truly a wonderful, genuine, and down-to-earth person.

Since that time, I have stayed in touch with Dennis. He invited me to visit the set of *Waterworld* in Hawaii to watch part of the filming. Dennis gave me a personal tour of parts of the set and invited me to have lunch in his trailer.

Now do you believe that it works? This relationship started because I took the initiative to introduce myself.

Introduce yourself to people, and stay in touch with everyone that you meet. This includes all teenage friends, high school friends, college friends, teachers, professors, sports teammates, business associates, your parents' friends, your relatives' friends, people you work with, people you work for - EVERYONE! You just never know where it could lead..........

Research Careers-NOW

> *"I was going to be a doctor because that's what my sister was. But I interned in a doctor's office when I was a teenager and learned that I hated it."*
>
> **-Stephanie Carolla**

A big part of your life will include your career. Do you have any idea what you want to do when you're out of school? You're not alone. I would bet that 90% of the teenagers in America have no clue!

You need to start getting a clue, now! You're not expected to know what will be your career for the rest of your life. But you do need to begin researching certain careers.

28

Why? Your life will revolve around your career. You will most likely work five days and 40 hours a week, 235 days and 2,040 hours a year, and about 7,000 days and 80,000 hours in your life. I bet you never thought of it like that.

How many times have you heard someone say, "I hate my job." You don't want to be in a situation where you hate going to work everyday.

But how do you choose a career? You start by identifying what makes you happy. If you identify the career that makes you happy you will begin to get a clear idea of what you may want to do when you get out of school.

Ask yourself the following two questions. They will help you to decide which career will make you happy:

1) Which career really excites and energizes me?

2) Which career would make me feel most fulfilled?

Once you begin to identify the career that makes you happy, make a commitment to yourself to pursue your ambition. Don't listen to those who try to discourage you. Many people dream of working a certain job or in a particular industry. But few accomplish their dreams because they listen when others tell them that it's not possible.

You have the ability to pursue and land any career you desire. Don't listen to those who try to discourage you. These are probably the very people who have never, and will never, have the career they desire. Just because they haven't done it, they think that you can't. They're wrong!

You need to start laying the foundation now. "So, how do I lay the foundation?" you ask. It's simple. You need to begin interning in the *Real World*. Work with your parents or teachers to arrange for you to go into various businesses to work for a day, week, month or even the entire summer. You will get an inside look at what it is really like to work in that career. You can't get this experience in a classroom or from a textbook. You will see what you like and dislike.

Tuleen Middleton is age 16 and lives in Los Angeles. Recently, I received a telephone call from Tuleen. She wanted to visit my office for the day to find out what it is like be a Stockbroker. I was very impressed that she had taken the initiative to ask if she could intern for the day. Naturally, I agreed.

Tuleen learned about different investments, how the industry operates and what happens in an office. One thing that really impressed me about Tuleen is that she carried a notebook the entire day. As we discussed certain areas of the industry, she would take notes. In addition, she asked many thoughtful questions.

Tuleen's internship provided her with important *Real World* information that just can't be learned in school.

Internships will improve your communication skills, provide you with experience and build your contacts. Remember to put your contacts in your address book, and stay in touch forever!

My first internship was the result of someone I knew from an early age. My first internship led to my second internship which led to my first job offer out of college. Take the initiative to intern. It's a small price to pay now, for a huge payoff later when you enter the *Real World*. You just never know where it could lead!

The Truth About Success and $

> *"We screwed our kids up. We taught them that the only way you can become successful is if you make a lot of money."*
>
> **-Charles Barkley**
> **NBA All-Star Player**

You need to understand a few things about success and money. First of all, having money does not mean you are successful. Drug dealers have a lot of money, big homes and drive fancy cars. Does that mean they are successful? NO! There is much more to success than having money.

One of the best definitions of success I have ever heard came from legendary UCLA basketball coach *John Wooden.* Coach Wooden's definition of success is:

> *"Peace of mind which is a direct result of self-satisfaction in knowing you did your best to become the best that you are capable of becoming."*

That's what success is all about, feeling good about yourself because you know that you did your best. Success is all about happiness. Happiness with yourself and your life.

There is nothing wrong with wanting to have money. The problem exists when you make money your main focus. You become greedy; your life becomes twisted. If you work hard and do what makes you happy, then money will follow.

"Money doesn't grow on trees!" How many times have you heard adults say this? Did you ever think they were right? Well, they are.

Since it doesn't grow on trees, shouldn't you keep what you have? Most teenagers think that spending is a hobby, and they can always squeeze another twenty out of others. I have news for you. Other people will not always be there to play Mr. and Mrs. Bank Teller. There will come a time in the very near future when you will be responsible for earning and managing your own money. You will soon find out that spending is not as much fun when it's your own money. It's time to learn some basic principles of good money management.

Saving

When you save money you do not spend it. That's right, no spending! By this I mean no more $120 sneakers, no more $100

CD player, no more $60 Jeans, and no more $50 concert tickets. The idea of saving is to keep more than you spend. The more you can save now, the more you will have later.

The problem is most teenagers don't have much self- control when it comes to saving money. Listed below are a few tips that will help you to save, at least a portion of what you have.

*   Put a portion of any money that you earn from working in a savings account at a bank. Ask your parents or an adult to help you open your own account.

*   Be a smart shopper. Do not just buy things for the fun of it. Buy only what is necessary ($120 sneakers are not necessary).

*   Leave your money at home when going to the mall or to stores. You are more likely to spend money when in the mall or stores. You can always go home to get money if there is something you absolutely need to buy.

*   Follow the "Golden Rule" to becoming wealthy. Take 10% of anything that you earn and put it away forever. This means that you never touch it unless it's an extreme emergency (Buying a new Nintendo tape is not an emergency). If you will continue to put 10% away from every paycheck for the next 20-30 years you will become very wealthy.

According to an article written in USA Weekend, Macaulay Culkin earned around $5 million for starring in the movie Home Alone 2, but he didn't spend any of it. The money went into a trust for him that he could have access to at an older age. Very smart! The more you save now, the more you will have later.

Credit Cards

When I received my first credit card, I thought someone had just given me a $1,000. Little did I realize after spending all of it, that I would have to repay it. To make matters worse, I was charged interest. This meant I would repay more than the $1,000 I had spent. (Oops!)

Understand that charging items on a credit card is like taking a loan. It must be repaid, plus interest. It's not free money and could get you in serious financial trouble if you go on a spending spree. Listed below are a few tips to help you avoid financial destruction:

*   Only charge what you know you can pay off when the monthly bill arrives. Never charge your card to the maximum limit.

*   Keep the receipts from all purchases so you can keep track of how much you have charged.

Remember, credit is not free money. It is money you must repay, plus interest. The best way to use a credit card is not to use it!

Investing

Our old friend Mr. Webster, (dictionary) lists the definition of investing as "to put (money) into business, stocks, etc... in order to get a profit." When you invest, you are putting your money into something that you believe will grow. If it grows, you will receive more money back than you originally put in (invested).

One of the most common ways to invest is to purchase stocks of companies. The way to buy stocks is through a stockbroker. Buying a few shares of stocks at a young age is one of the best ways to get started learning about investing and the stock market.

A good way to begin investing is to buy stocks of companies whose products or services you use. The following are a few examples:

McDonald's	Disney	NIKE
Coca-Cola	Reebok	Sony
PepsiCo	Wendy's	Marvel
Microsoft	IBM	Apple

Ask yourself which products or services you and your friends use, then find out information on those companies. It may be worth buying a few shares if there is demand for their products or services.

Another investment vehicle is stock mutual funds. A stock mutual fund is like an Easter egg basket filled with eggs. The basket is the mutual fund and the eggs are the individual stocks. When you buy a mutual fund you own a piece of the stocks in your basket. How well the stocks in the fund do determines how well the overall fund performs. Mutual funds are a good way to diversify your risk because you own pieces of many stocks rather than just buying one stock. Some mutual fund companies will allow you to start investing with as little as $50 to $100.

How to Become a Millionaire

Forget about "get-rich-quick" schemes. The best way to create wealth is buy investing for the long term. The key is to start early.

If you are working as a teenager, great! If you are not, then you may want to consider getting a job so you can earn a little money to invest. Think about it. If you are like most teenagers, you probably live at home with your parents and have no bills or financial obligations. If you were to get a part-time job, you could earn enough to invest and begin creating your fortune. Consider the following example:

Suppose you were to get a part-time job and worked only 15 hours per week and got paid $5 per hour. You would earn $75 per week, $300 per month and $3,600 per year. Let's suppose that $600 of the $3,600 you earn a year is what you owe to Uncle Sam for income tax. That would leave you with $3,000 remaining.

Since you are working and have earned income, you can invest up to $2,000 a year in an Individual Retirement Account (IRA). An IRA is an account that allows you to put money into it to be used for your retirement. You do not pay any taxes on the growth of the money until it is withdrawn, usually between the ages of 60 to 65.

If you invest $2,000 a year from age 15 to 19, and never invest any more after age 19, (assuming your annual return of at least 12%) your money would be worth more than $1,000,000 by age 59 1/2.

Compounding interest creates a huge snowball effect. Your interest keeps accumulating over the years without losing a portion of your growth to income taxes.

If you withdraw any portion of your money before age 59 1/2, there is a 10% penalty on any money taken out and it is also subject to income tax.

If you take $2,000 of the $3,000 you earn from your part-time job and invest it in an IRA, and you do that from age 15 to 19 (5 years), you will become a millionaire. The following table illustrates how your money would grow.

Age	Year	Investment	15%	14%
15	1	$2,000	2,300	2,280
16	2	$2,000	4,945	4,879
17	3	$2,000	7,987	7,842
18	4	$2,000	11,485	11,220
19	5	$2,000	15,507	15,071
20	6	0	17,834	17,181
30	16	0	72,147	63,694
40	26	0	291,874	236,127
50	36	0	1,180,794	875,374
59	45	0	4,153,888	2,846,668

Age	Year	Investment	13%	12%
15	1	$2,000	2,260	2,240
16	2	$2,000	4,814	4,749
17	3	$2,000	7,700	7,559
18	4	$2,000	10,961	10,706
19	5	$2,000	14,645	14,230
20	6	0	16,549	15,938
30	16	0	56,176	49,501
40	26	0	190,696	153,743
50	36	0	647,328	477,502
59	45	0	1,944,602	1,324,150

(The author is only offering ideas and suggestions for investing. He is not promising or guaranteeing any investment returns or performance and is not liable for any losses that may occur to your investments. Consult your parents or a licensed financial advisor before starting any investing.)

> *"I found the road to wealth when I decided that a part of all I earn was mine to keep."*
>
> **-George S. Clason**

Never Stop Learning

> *"An open mind is the beginning of self-discovery and growth. We can't learn anything new until we can admit that we don't already know anything."*
>
> -Erwin G. Hall

I'm sure you have heard the phrase *Knowledge is Power!* How true this is. The more you learn, the more you grow. The more you grow, the more diverse your background becomes. The more diverse your background becomes, the more valuable you will be.

The problem with most people is they think they know it all. People who know it all are stopping themselves from learning. When you think you know it all your mind isn't open to new ideas and opinions.

> *"It's what you know after you know it all that counts."*
> **-John Wooden**
> **legendary UCLA basketball coach**

To become more valuable and interesting, open your mind to new ideas and opinions. Make it a point to learn something new everyday, whether in or out of school.

It's not only important to pay attention in school, but also outside of school as well. Pay attention to current events that are happening in everyday life. Take the initiative to keep learning.

But how can you do this? It's easy - *communicate and listen, write, read,* and *watch TV*. Let's start with communicating and listening, since the two go hand in hand.

Communicate and Listen

> *"You have two ears and one mouth. They should be used in that proportion."*
> **-Unknown**

You are communicating with people everyday of your life. Every time you communicate with someone you have the opportunity to learn something new if you will listen. Most people communicate and never listen. They want to talk and get their own opinions out.

Talk to a variety of people. People of different ages, nationalities and backgrounds. Don't be intimidated because they may be a little different than you.

It's easy to get people talking. Simply ask them questions. People love talking about themselves, especially if they feel they are teaching you how to do something. It makes them feel important. Questions always can start a conversation and keep it going. Never be scared to ask people questions. That's how you learn.

> *"One thing I consistently do is communicate with different people. One percent of what I learn everyday is from talking with people. The other 99% is from listening to them."*
>
> -James Malinchak

Writing

Another great way to learn is by *writing*. This includes letters, research papers, and even a book! One of my favorite exercises that I have teenagers do in my seminars is called the *"Learn About Myself"* exercise. Try it, you'll be amazed at what you will learn about yourself. Write the following on a piece of paper, then answer them honestly.

1) Which five things do I most value in my life?
2) Which five goals are most important to me?
3) Who are the five most important people in my life?
4) What would I do if I won $1,000,000 today?
5) What would I do if I only had 6 months to live?
6) Which one thing would I try if I knew I could not fail?
7) Which one thing would I change about the world?

You don't need to show your answers to anyone. The exercise is to help you learn about yourself. Do this exercise at least once a year. Your answers will probably change every year.

Reading

> *"I always turn to the sports page first.....it records people's accomplishments; the front page, nothing but man's failure."*
> **-Earl Warren**
> **former Chief Justice**
> **United States Supreme Court**

I agree with Earl Warren that you should read the sports page. But I also feel you need to read every other part of the paper as well. Remember, your goal is to become more diverse. You never know when you will be in a situation where you need to discuss a current event. If you only focus on reading one part of the paper, it could make you feel uncomfortable in certain situations. Here's an example:

Last year, I was in Chicago at a convention promoting another book that I had written. I was eating breakfast and reading the morning newspaper. Actually, I was only reading the sports page. To me, the sports page seemed to be the most important and interesting and I figured I could get by without reading the other sections.

A friend came up to me and asked if I would like to hear First Lady Hillary Clinton speak and meet her afterwards. "Absolutely!" I replied.

I put down the sports page and went to the speech. Half of her speech focused on book writing and the other half focused on raising children properly.

After her speech my friend took me into a private area where we were able to meet and talk with Mrs. Clinton. As I began talking with her, she asked if I had read the article in the morning paper on raising children. Oops! I was speechless.

Read all parts of the newspaper. You never know when you may be in a situation that requires a discussion of a current event. You may even be quizzed by the First Lady!

I also recommend that you read magazines and books. It's been proven that you can increase your knowledge and vocabulary simply by reading. Keep a dictionary nearby when you read. If you don't understand a word, don't just breeze by it. Take a minute to look it up and understand the definition. You will be learning a new word.

Watch TV

Have your parents ever complained that you watch too much TV? They're not entirely wrong. TV is OK, if watched in moderation. You don't want to waste your life by becoming a couch potato.

TV is great if you can learn from what you are watching. I'm not saying you shouldn't watch the no-nonsense sitcoms. Hey, I love *Seinfield*. Kramer's the man! And every week you can find me in front of the tube watching *Friends*.

What I am simply trying to get across to you is that there are certain times when you need to "watch-to-learn." Just as you read the newspaper to keep up to speed on current events, you should also watch the local or world news. It only takes 30 minutes a day to get updated on the most important stories.

In addition to the news, there are other quality programs that can serve as informative and educational outlets such as PBS and The Discovery Channel.

I am not telling you not to watch movies either. I am one of the biggest movie buffs you will ever meet. If I'm not going out to catch the latest flick, you can always find me at home with a video rental. There are certain movies that everyone can learn from. Here are a few that can teach you some important success principles:

Rocky I & II:
Sylvester Stallone plays boxer Rocky Balboa who gets a chance to fight Apollo Creed for the World Heavyweight Boxing Title. No one gave him a chance. But no matter how bad Rocky was beaten up or how many times he was knocked down in the fight, he kept getting up. In Rocky II, he became the Heavyweight Champion and proved that you can accomplish your dreams if you simply "go for it" and keep getting up when you're knocked down.

Rudy:
This is a movie about a student who enrolled at the University of Notre Dame and tried out for the football team. His dream was to play one play in a real game, but he was much smaller than the other players and not as athletic. He never lost focus of his dream. Finally, he got the chance to play, sacked the quarterback, and at the end of the game, he was carried off the field on the shoulders of his teammates. No other player since "Rudy" has ever been carried off the field at the University of Notre Dame. It's a great movie about pursuing your dreams and not quitting.

Cool Runnings:

This movie is about a group of guys from Jamaica whose one goal is to compete in the bobsled event at the Winter Olympics. They were laughed at by people around the world and even by high ranking officials of their own country. After all, how could a team from the tropical island of Jamaica compete in a winter sport against teams who live in snow, ice and cold weather all year around. They didn't care if no one believed in them. All that mattered was that they believed in themselves. They did compete in the Winter Olympics and won the respect of people around the world. A great movie about believing in yourself and not listening to those who tell you that you can't do something.

> *"The greatest investment of all is in yourself. No one can take an education from you. Learn everything you can. Buy a dictionary and study one page every day. Understanding words is a key to success."*
> **-Dr. Leroy Perry**

Always Believe
in Yourself

> *"The mind is the limit. As long as the mind can envision the fact that you can do something, you can do it - as long as you really believe it 100%."*
>
> **-Arnold Schwarzenegger**

Believing in yourself is the most important habit you must adopt in life. As you journey through life you will meet people who tell you that you're not smart enough to succeed. You will meet people who tell you that you don't have the ability to succeed. And you will certainly meet people who just don't believe in you or your abilities. So if you don't believe in yourself and the dreams you desire, then who will?

A great story of believing in yourself is that of **Ron Rice,** founder of Hawaiian Tropic sun tanning oils and lotions. He grew up in a log cabin in North Carolina and worked his way through college as a lifeguard.

Ron's idea began as a mixture of a few ingredients in a garbage can in his garage. Today, Hawaiian Tropic is one of the largest tanning oil and lotion manufacturers in the world, grossing hundreds of millions of dollars each year.

> *"My mother taught me very early to believe I could achieve any accomplishment I wanted to. The first was to walk without braces."*
>
> **-Wilma Rudolph**
> **winner of three Olympic gold medals**

At age 4, **Wilma Rudolph** contracted scarlet fever and double pneumonia, which left her with a paralyzed leg. She had to wear a metal leg brace until age nine. At age 13, she entered a race and came in last place. Everyone told her to quit running, but she didn't. She believed in herself and continued until she finally won a race. She continued running and kept on winning. Eventually she went on to win three Olympic gold medals. This was the same little girl who was told she would never walk again.

How about the story of **Michael Jordan?** Did you know that Michael Jordan was once cut from his high school basketball team? It would have been easy for Michael to begin to feel sorry for himself and to stop believing in his ability. But he didn't! He didn't listen to those who told him he would fail or those who laughed at him. He simply continued believing in himself and didn't quit until he had accomplished his goals.

Look where he is today. Michael Jordan is probably the most famous athlete on the planet. Where do you think he would be had he given up and quit believing in himself when he was cut from his high school team?

Train Your Mind

> *"Whether you think you can or think you can't - you are right."*
>
> **-Henry Ford**

Nothing can be achieved unless you <u>first</u> believe it. Train your mind to believe that you WILL achieve your dreams.

Your brain is a muscle. Like any other muscle in your body, it needs to be exercised in order for it to grow, become stronger and increase its performance. The way to accomplish this is through proper exercise of your muscle (brain).

I'm sure that most of you have heard of ***Bill Gates.*** If you haven't then you probably have at least used computer software designed by his company, Microsoft. Bill Gates is listed as the richest man in America with an estimated net worth of $50 billion. (That's right, billion!)

In a recent interview, Bill was asked how he is able to develop unique ideas and concepts that continuously put Microsoft ahead of all other computer software companies. His answer was amazing, but simple.

Bill told a story of his childhood. He said that one day his mother could not find him anywhere in the house. Finally, she opened the closet door and found him sitting there in the dark closet. When his mother asked him why he was sitting in a dark closet, he replied, "I'm thinking."

Bill went on in the interview to stress how important it is to exercise your brain because it responds to repetitive exercise.

> *"The key to success is to study. Your brain must be exercised like a muscle - work it well."*
>
> **-Joe Weider**
> **Chairman of the Board, Weider Publications**
> **creator of Muscle & Fitness magazine**

There's a quotation that says, *"Repetition is the Mother of Skill,"* meaning that in order for you to improve or increase performance, you need to practice the fundamentals over and over again.

Studies have indicated that it takes approximately 21-30 days to create a new habit. This means that if you want to change or create a belief in your mind, it should become a natural habit after working on it for 21-30 days.

> *"We are what we repeatedly do. Excellence, then, is not an act, but a habit."*
>
> **-Aristotle**

Have a Positive Attitude

Your attitude is crucial in determining whether you succeed or fail. Your attitude is the foundation of the ideas that are formed in your mind. Your mind is like a computer. It accepts anything that you focus on. What you focus on, is what you become and achieve. Don't make negative statements or think negative thoughts, because your brain will store them in your memory (just like a computer) and never forget them.

If you continuously store negative thoughts in your brain, you will eventually become a negative, non-achieving person. It may not be today, tomorrow or next week. But be assured that one day it will happen to you.

Begin right here, right now to make only positive statements and to think only positive thoughts. To get the results you desire in life, change your thoughts. What you focus on, you will achieve, because thoughts are transformed into results. If you change the way you think, then you can change the person you become. Anything that happens in life first begins as a thought.

Elevate your attitude to elevate your success. Many people never reach their full potential because they never develop a strong mental attitude. They think negative thoughts rather than positive thoughts. It's simple - think positive thoughts if you want positive results.

Positive Attitude   =   Positive Results
Negative Attitude   =   Negative Results

Start right now to develop a positive attitude and begin focusing your thoughts on believing in yourself and your abilities. Before you realize it you will be accomplishing whatever you believe.

Get Up When Life Knocks You Down

"If I were asked to give what I consider the single most useful bit of advice for all humanity it would be this: Expect trouble as an inevitable part of life and when it comes, hold your head high, look it squarely in the eye and say, I will be bigger than you. You cannot defeat me."

-Ann Landers

As you go through life, you will be faced with many roadblocks. Obstacles that will knock you down. How successful you become in life will depend on your willingness to get up when life knocks you down.

You will be knocked down, because it happens to everyone. It's a part of life. The question is, who will get up? Those who get up when they are knocked down and those who continuously overcome obstacles succeed in life.

> ## *"Success is how high you bounce after you hit bottom."*
> ### -General George S. Patton

The next time you get knocked down and want to complain about how life isn't treating you fairly, or whenever you start thinking about quitting and giving up, remember a few of these people:

When **Heather Whitestone** was 18 months old, she lost her full hearing in one ear and about 95% in the other ear. She was forced to learn to read lips as a child in order to communicate with others. Her entire life was difficult, living daily with her hearing disability. Despite being hearing impaired since her childhood, Heather didn't let it stand in the way of achieving her dreams.

In September 1994, Heather Whitestone went on to win the crown of *Miss America*, becoming the first person with a physical disability to win the title in the pageant's history. Although her disability presented her with many obstacles in her life, she never quit pursuing her dreams.

> ## *"An obstacle is what you see when you take your eyes off of your goals and dreams."*
> ### -Unknown

Jim Abbott is a major league baseball player. What you may not know is that he has only one hand. Most people would not only give up on baseball, but also life, if they had only one hand. It would have been easy for him to feel sorry for himself and give up. But not Jim. He wasn't going to allow this obstacle to stand in the way of his dream of playing professional baseball. He looked at the good qualities that he had and focused his mind on accomplishing his dream. Today, Jim Abbott is one of the top Pitchers in professional baseball.

> *"An obstacle is only an obstacle if you allow it to be an obstacle."*
>
> **-Unknown**

The horrifying experience of *Jackie Pflug* is one of the most inspirational stories you will ever hear. Jackie was a passenger on Egyptian Air Flight 648 a few years ago. The flight was going along as normal when suddenly the plane was hijacked by terrorists. During the hijacking one of the terrorists shot her in the head and left her for dead. But Jackie wasn't ready to die. She did not stop fighting for her life. Even when the odds on living seemed impossible, she still never gave up. Because of her determination to live, she miraculously survived and now spends her time traveling the country inspiring others to overcome obstacles in their lives.

> *"Success seems to be largely a matter of hanging on after others have let go."*
>
> **-Unknown**

On June 2, 1995, *Scott O'Grady*, a U.S. Air Force Captain, was flying the skies over Bosnia when his F-16 aircraft was unexpectedly hit with a Soviet-made missile. As his plane was burning and getting ready to explode, Scott pulled the ejection handle and flew five miles up from his plane, traveling at a rate of 350 miles per hour. (Approximately five times as fast as the average 55 mph freeway traffic travels.) He landed safely in the jungles of Bosnia. But his troubles were just beginning.

Scott was stranded for six days and nights with no food or supplies while he was hunted by the Bosnian soldiers trying to capture him. Many times the soldiers were as close as five feet from him. But Scott relied on his faith in God, his family and friends, and his confidence to escape to safety and eventually to return to the U.S. He never allowed his incredibly difficult situation to defeat him.

> *"Persistence means taking pains to overcome every obstacle, and to do what's necessary to reach your goals."*
> **-Unknown**

Dennis Bird was a star defensive lineman for the New York Jets. In a regular season game, Dennis made a routine move to get in position to sack the opposing team's quarterback. As he lunged to make the sack, one of his teammates lunged at the quarterback from the opposite side. He and Dennis collided with such a tremendous impact that it left Dennis lying on the field, paralyzed from the neck down. Doctors told him that he would never walk again. No matter how dark the outlook or how many doctors told him that he was crippled for life, Dennis remained positive and told everyone that he would not quit fighting until he walked again.

Many months later, Dennis walked onto the field to a standing ovation before a Jets game.

Dan Jansen had been labeled "the heartbreak kid" of the winter Olympics. He was expected to win a gold medal for the United States in speed skating. Only hours before his race in Calgary at the 1988 winter games, Dan received terrible news. His sister, Jane, had just died of leukemia. With the death of his sister on his mind, Dan was unable to concentrate and fell during his race, losing the opportunity to win a gold medal.

Dan could have given in to the obstacle and quit, but he didn't. He worked for a chance to compete for the gold in the 1994 Olympics in Lillehammer, Norway. After again falling several times, Dan accomplished his dream. In the final race of his career, Dan dug up the inner strength to beat the odds. He won the gold medal!

To top off his amazing story, while winning the gold medal he set an all-time record for 1,000-meter speed skating and was proclaimed *"The Greatest Sprinter on Long Blades in the past decade!"*

Dan is living proof that if you continue to get up when life knocks you down you can achieve anything!

> *"Always have passion for life and never stop trying. The secret is to never give up!"*
>
> **-Bob Del Montique**
> **International Fitness Expert**

Hard Work Pays Off

> *"Opportunity is missed by most people because it is dressed in overalls and looks like work."*
> -Thomas Edison

I have a great father! He is the hardest working man I have ever known in my life. Whether it was working at his job on the railroad or doing the yard work, he always gave 110%.

Aside from his railroad job he had a weekend job. He was a NCAA Division 1 college football official. Many of you may have yelled at him for calling a penalty on your favorite college team. He officiated games that included Notre Dame, Miami (FL), Penn State, Pittsburgh, Army, Navy, Texas, USC, Tennessee, North Carolina, Syracuse, Florida and Boston College to name a few.

In December 1987, he was rated one of the top five college football officials in the entire nation and was selected to officiate the Orange Bowl game for the National Championship. The game was between the Oklahoma Sooners and the Miami Hurricanes live, on

ABC nationwide TV. In case you are wondering, Miami won the game and became the National Champions.

A few days after the game, I did what most teenage guys do after a big sporting event, I read Sports Illustrated. The cover story was written about Miami winning the National Championship. As I flipped through the pages I came to the big spread of pictures of the game. The first picture I saw was that of my father. I couldn't believe it. I was so excited and began telling everyone that my dad was in Sports Illustrated.

I was very proud of my father's accomplishments because we lived in a very small town, and it was my dad who was achieving all of this. It wasn't a person from a big city like Los Angeles or New York. It was my dad from the little town of Monessen, PA.

I sat back for minute and began trying to figure out how he accomplished all that he did. Suddenly it hit me. My entire life I remember my father telling me one thing over and over. He would say, *"Jim, you have to work hard for the things you want in life because hard work always pays off."*

That is such a true statement. How else could he accomplish his officiating goals? Hard work did pay off for him.

Fortunately, I paid attention to his credo of *"hard work always pays off."* The problem most teenagers have is that they don't listen when their parents try to advise them.

I decided to dedicate myself to working extremely hard to get a basketball scholarship. My philosophy was simple: There may be players who run faster or jump higher, but no one would work harder than me. People started calling me a gym-rat. (That's a nice term for workaholic.)

In the summer I would attend camps, run, lift weights and play in recreational leagues everyday. Sometimes I would work out two or three times a day.

When school began, I made friends with a few of the janitors who would open the school early in the morning. They agreed to let me in before school started.

I arrived at the gym at 6:00 A.M. everyday to work on my shooting, passing and ball handling for 1 1/2 hours before school. Then I would shower and go to school. After school, it was off to the weight room for 2 hours of weight lifting. After lifting, it was back in the gym for another 1 1/2 hours of drills.

By the time the season rolled around, my strength, endurance and skill level was much higher than that of any opposing player. I truly believe that my relentless work ethic, was one of the main reasons that I achieved almost every basketball goal I had set for myself, including receiving a NCAA Division 1 scholarship!

Thanks Dad! You were right, *"Hard Work Always Pays Off!"*

The thrill of achieving a goal is knowing that you put in the time and worked hard for it. Whether it's receiving an "A" in school, getting an academic or athletic scholarship, landing a great job, earning a million dollars, helping a charity, or whatever. The satisfaction of knowing that it was your dedication, your commitment, and your effort is what makes achieving a goal worthwhile.

> *"Genius is one percent inspiration and ninety-nine percent perspiration."*
> **-Thomas Edison**

Nothing great in life can be accomplished without working hard for it. I have a friend in Los Angeles named **Dr. Leroy Perry.** Many people consider him the top chiropractor in the world. He is an inventor, writer and health educator who is a specialist in teaching patients self-help. He was the first chiropractor in history to be an official Olympic doctor and has officially served in five Olympics. His patients include many movie stars, professional athletes and top level business executives. He treats Madonna, Jack Nicholson, Sharon Stone, Shirley MacLaine, Wilt Chamberlain and Elizabeth Taylor to name a few.

Look up the term *hard worker* in the dictionary, and you'll find the definition "Dr. Perry." He works early mornings, late evenings and on weekends. He even makes house calls to those patients who are not able to visit his office. I guess this is the very reason he is one of the best in the world at what he does.

One day I asked Dr. Perry why he works as hard as he does. His answer is something we all need to realize. Dr. Perry said, *"There is no free lunch in this world! You have to work hard to achieve your goals. If you want something, go after it and never quit until you get it."*

Dr. Perry hit the nail on the head. Successful people understand the importance of working hard to achieve their goals. The most successful people in society are some of the hardest workers.

Larry Bird is one of the greatest basketball players ever to play the game. He led the Boston Celtics to consecutive NBA titles while earning numerous awards, including Most Valuable Player (MVP) of the league.

Larry had many outstanding accomplishments in his career but he never had the athletic ability or talent that some other NBA players had. So he dedicated himself to work harder than anyone else. He would be the first player on the floor before practice and the last to leave when practice was finished. When no other players were in the gym, Larry was there practicing and working hard to improve his game. He knew that he could not continue to achieve his goals without his work ethic.

> *"One hundred percent is not enough; the world belongs to those who aim for 110%."*
> **-George Allen**
> **former head football coach**
> **Washington Redskins**

Remember my friend *Michael Moorer.* He defeated Evander Holyfield to become the World Heavyweight Boxing Champion. This achievement may not seem impressive, for you may not know of Michael's background.

Michael and I grew up in a small steel mill town, Monessen, near Pittsburgh, PA. Our town has a population of 9,000 people. The odds of someone coming from that background becoming a world champion are slim.

Winter in Western Pennsylvania can be brutal. At times it would be as cold as 10 degrees below zero, but Michael would be out running in the streets. When his friends were going out on Friday and Saturday nights to have a good time, Michael was going to the gym to hit a speed bag.

The most impressive thing that I can remember about Michael is that he constantly worked out. One day when we were about age 15, I asked him how he could work out 3 hours a day, 5-7 days a week? His answer taught me a very important lesson in life at a young age. Michael said that his goal was to become the World Heavyweight Boxing Champion and the only way he could achieve that, with all the odds against him, was to work harder than anyone.

That's what working hard is all about. You set a goal, make a commitment, then work hard to achieve it. If you desire to achieve a goal, then be willing put in the time. Many times you will have to work harder or longer. But it is well worth it!

> *"There is no substitute for work. It is the price of success."*
>
> **-Earl Blaik**
> **former football coach, West Point**

Make the Right Choices

> *"My basic principle is that you don't make decisions because they are easy, you don't make them because they're cheap, you don't make them because they're popular; you make them because they are right."*
>
> **-Theodore M. Hesburgh, C.S.C.**
> **President, University of Notre Dame**

Decisions are so powerful. Each decision you make everyday will shape your future. Making one wrong choice can change your life forever. The problem with making decisions is most people think "IT will never happen to me!" IT can happen to you, whatever IT may be. Just look at the man known as "Magic."

Earvin "Magic" Johnson of the Los Angeles Lakers is one of the greatest basketball players ever to play the game. He was strong, healthy and at the top of his game. Nothing could go wrong, right? Wrong!

Everything in Magic's life changed in the Fall of 1991 when a routine physical revealed that he had contracted HIV, the virus that causes AIDS. In a split second, his entire life changed.

Magic made the choice not to be in a monogamous relationship. The wrong choice he made affected his life, the lives of his family and friends, his teammates, and the lives of millions of people worldwide. Hopefully, he also affected your life.

If there is one positive result that came from Magic tragically contracting HIV, it is that more people, especially teenagers, have become aware that anyone can catch the disease. Anyone, even you!

Sex is not a game. More teenagers are contracting HIV every year. Consider the following facts that were taken from a recent letter written to teachers by Dr. Ernest Fleishman, Director of Education of Scholastic Inc. and Dr. Charles Schuster, Director of the National Institute of Drug Abuse:

*   The spread of HIV - the virus that causes AIDS - is increasing rapidly among teenagers. According to the Centers for Disease Control (CDC), the number of diagnosed teenagers with AIDS rose 96 percent over the past two years.

*   Today, people in their 20s account for one out of every five AIDS cases. Because HIV infection can take many years to develop into AIDS, a large number of these people probably were infected when they were teenagers.

Do yourself a favor by learning the facts about HIV and AIDS. Listed below are a few hotlines you can call and get free information. Anything that you discuss with a counselor is confidential. Don't be shy; one simple phone call could save your life.

*   *The National AIDS Hotline* (1-800-342-AIDS)
      Answers questions confidentially about AIDS.

*   *The Sexually Transmitted Disease (STD) Hotline*
      Answers questions confidentially about sexually
      transmitted diseases and offers pamphlets.
      Call toll-free: 1-800-227-8922

In addition to requesting information from the hotlines, go to your local bookstore and buy the following book. (If it is not in stock, have the bookstore order it for you.) It gives the facts about AIDS and is written for teenagers:

Risky Times: How to be AIDS-Smart & Stay Healthy - A Guide for Teenagers, by Jeanne Blake. New York: Workman, 1990, $5.95.

Stay Away From Drugs

> *"Drugs do nothing but kill! They kill your body, they kill your mind, and they can kill YOU!"*
>
> **-James Malinchak**

What can you possibly gain from using drugs? Drugs can do nothing positive for your life. They cause people to self-destruct. Just as a time bomb will explode, so will your mind, body, and your life if you choose to be friends with drugs.

According to The U.S. Department of Education, a 16-year-old girl told doctors that her entire life was focused on crack. The amazing thing about this is that she was interviewed on a Friday and had used crack for the first time the previous Monday. Within five days the drug had completely taken over her life!

Don't try to justify using drugs by saying that everyone is doing it, and that if you do it, you will be cool. Cool with your friends and the more popular kids. You will not be cool...you will be stupid!

Do you think you will be cool if you mess with drugs and get kicked out of school? If you get kicked out of school, you will have difficulty being accepted to any college and you may never be able to land a good job. Once you get an "F" grade on your "life report card" for messing with drugs, it can't be erased. But you *can* turn your life around. If you're messing with drugs, simply *make the choice* to stop.

Do you think you will be cool if you mess with drugs and jump out of a window because you think you could fly? It happens.

Drugs can cause you to do things that you normally wouldn't do. They may cause you to hurt or even kill someone. They can even kill you. Do you want to take the chance of dying just to get a cheap high?

Think Before You Do Drugs

> *"You don't do drugs. Drugs do you!"*
>
> **-Eddie Jones**
> **Los Angeles Lakers**
> **for Drug Free Southern California**

Don't get high on drugs, get high on life. Get high from doing fun things with your friends. Get high from getting love from your family. Get high from making good grades in school. Get high from succeeding in sports. The positive things in life can give you a much better high than drugs. You don't need drugs to enjoy yourself.

Your parents, brothers and sisters, friends, boyfriend or girlfriend, teachers nor anyone else can make you stay away from drugs. Only you can make the choice. The choice is yours.

I can't make you stay away from drugs. All I ask is that you think before you do drugs. Think before you give in to the evil of drugs. Think about your family. Think about your friends. Think about how empty their lives would be if you were to die from messing with drugs. If you think that you can't die because you're young and healthy then think again.

Len Bias was a number one NBA draft pick who was about to sign a multimillion-dollar contract. He was expected to become one of the greatest basketball players ever to play for the Boston Celtics.

The night he was drafted by the Celtics Len Bias made the choice to use drugs and he died. He never earned any of the multimillion-dollars. He never had the chance to become one of the Celtics all time great players. Len Bias was a strong and healthy individual, probably in much better condition than you. If he could die from drugs, you certainly can also!

Alcohol Is A Drug

> *"We must teach our children that alcohol is a drug."*
>
> **-former President George Bush**

Many of you do not realize that alcohol is, also, a drug. It impairs your thinking, reflexes and ability to make rational choices. Alcohol abuse can lead to medical problems, unplanned pregnancies, suicide attempts, crimes such as assault and rape, and AIDS. Consider the following facts that were recently reported by SADD (Students Against Destructive Decisions):

* One in three college students now drink primarily to get drunk.

* 95% of violent crime on campus is alcohol related.

* 90% of all reported campus rapes occur when alcohol is being used by either the assailant or the victim or both.

* 60% of college women who have acquired STD's, sexually transmitted diseases, including AIDS and genital herpes, were under the influence of alcohol at the time they had intercourse.

If these facts haven't fazed you, then maybe the following incidents will help you to realize the terrible, and in some cases, fatal effect alcohol can have on you. They were reported by the U.S. Center for Substance Abuse Prevention:

* A Southwest Missouri State University freshman died after jumping off a seventh-story building balcony during spring break on South Padre Island. Police said the student was tampering with a fire hose when a security guard confronted him. The student ran down a corridor and threw himself over the balcony. An autopsy showed that the 18-year-old student had been drinking.

* An Eastern Illinois University student who had fallen into a lime pit was hospitalized with second- and third- degree chemical burns over 63% of his body. The 20-year-old junior was found lying unconscious and said he had been drinking and could not remember how he got into the lime.

* A 19-year-old Lewis University student fatally shot himself with a .38 caliber revolver in a game of Russian roulette. According to his roommate, the student had apparently spun the chamber and pulled the trigger several times before the round fired, killing him instantly. Both students had been drinking prior to the incident.

* An 18-year-old University of Colorado freshman was killed after being thrown from the roof of a vehicle. The 18-year-old driver who had been drinking, as had all four passengers, tried to take a curve too fast and went off the side of the road, rolling the vehicle on its top.

> *"The greatest power that a person possesses is the power to choose."*
>
> **-J. Martin Kohe**

> *"Drunk driving is one of the most deadly scourges ever to strike modern times and it is as crippling as crack, as random as gang violence, and it's killing more kids than both combined....."*
>
> **-former President George Bush**

Don't screw up your life. *Make the right choices!*

Take time to learn more facts about drugs and alcohol. Listed below are a few organizations you need to contact that will provide you with the necessary information:

* *SADD (Students Against Driving Drunk)*
  P.O. Box 800 - Marlboro, MA 01752
  (508) 481-3568 - Fax (508) 481-5759

* *Just Say No Foundation*
  1777 N. California Blvd.-Walnut Creek, CA 94596
  1-800-258-2766

* *Alcoholics Anonymous Worldwide Services, Inc.*
  475 Riverside Drive - New York, NY 10115
  (212) 870-3400

Be Thankful for What You Have

> *"Don't complain because you don't have.*
> *Enjoy what you've got."*
>
> **-H. Stanley Judd**

It is said that everyone should have an inspiration in their life. It may be a motivational talk from someone you respect, an experience that you have or a book that you read. (Like this book!) Whatever the inspiration, it teaches you to look at life from a different perspective.

My inspiration came from my sister Vicki. She was warm, kind and caring. She didn't care about accolades or being written up in newspapers. All she wanted was to share her love with the people she cared about, her family and friends. She had the positive qualities that would bring out the best in anyone.

About a month before I was to depart for my junior year of college, Vicki collapsed one evening with the right side of her body paralyzed. The initial indication was that she had suffered a stroke. However, test results confirmed it was much more serious.

There was a malignant brain tumor causing her paralysis. Her doctors didn't give her more than three months to live. I remember wondering how this could happen? A few weeks before she collapsed Vicki was perfectly fine. And now her life was coming to an end at a young age.

The day before my scheduled departure I had mixed emotions about leaving. Part of me said to forget about college and stay there with Vicki. The other part said to finish my education. I was unsure about what to do.

It was getting late and I had to make a decision. Only Vicki and I were in her hospital room. I made the mistake of telling her that I might not leave for college. She became angry and told me I had better finish my education. Vicki said that she would be fine and not to worry about her. There was Vicki lying ill in a hospital bed telling me not to worry.

Leaving that evening, knowing it was the last time I would see her alive was the most difficult thing I have ever done. Before leaving, Vicki made me promise never to give up fighting against any obstacle in my life. Again, there she was lying ill in a hospital bed encouraging me. It didn't seem fair that such a wonderful person had to go through this agony.

Vicki passed away on November 29, 1991 living a month longer than her doctors had expected her to live. The doctors couldn't give an explanation of how she overcame the odds and lived this long.

They didn't have to because I already knew the answer. She did it because she never gave up fighting to overcome her obstacle.....

Vicki inspired me never to give up even if the odds seem impossible. If you believe you will win then you will. Vicki proved that by living longer than she was expected to live. She won! And because of her I know I will win against any obstacle I face.

This experience taught me what's really important in life, your faith, good health and safety, the people you love and care about, and the ability to pursue your dreams. I am very thankful for having all of these and do not take them for granted.

Take a minute to think about who is important in your life, then tell them that you love them and care about them. Be thankful for what you have. You may wake up one day and have a piece of it missing.

Appreciate Your Parents and Loved Ones

"I don't believe athletes should be role models. I believe parents should be role models...Kids idolize professional athletes, which is wrong in itself...To kids that idolize me, I tell them don't do it just because I can dribble a basketball - that's really sick."

-Charles Barkley
NBA All-Star Player

How many times have you complained that your parents or guardians are getting on your case? Have you ever said you can't stand them and can't wait until you no longer live in their house?

Think about something. Why do you think that they wait up for you when you're out late? Why do they tell you to be home at a certain time? It's not because they're on your case. It's because they love and care about you.

The next time your parents or guardians are waiting up for you or tell you to be home at a certain time, thank them. Tell them that you appreciate the fact that they care about you enough to worry.

I have never met one person in my entire life who doesn't want to be cared for and loved. Imagine if no one cared. There are many teenagers in the world who don't have loving parents or guardians. Many teenagers are beaten daily or sexually abused.

Appreciate your parents and loved ones. Tell them that you love, respect and care about them. The problem with most teenagers is that they take their parents and those who care about them for granted. They don't realize what their loved ones may have sacrificed and done for them throughout the years.

> *"If loving and respecting your mother and being proud of her makes you a mama's boy, then that's what I am."*
>
> **-Charles Barkley**

Earlier I mentioned that my father taught me that "hard work always pays off" and that his example was an important factor in my athletic success. My mother was equally as important to my success. She provided love, encouragement and emotional support.

Remember when I mentioned that I would get to school at 6:00 A.M. every morning to work on my basketball skills? Who do you think drove me there? My Mother! Not only did she drive me, she also made sure that I got out of bed every morning, had a nice breakfast and clean clothes. She sacrificed a lot because she cared about helping me to succeed. That is something that I will always appreciate and remember.

"Thank you, Mom! I really appreciate it!"

Stop reading for a few minutes and think about all of the little things that your loved ones have sacrificed for you. How have they gone out of their way to help you? Show them you appreciate them by telling them thank you and that you love them. Do it now, you never know what may happen tomorrow. They may not be around.

Strive for Good Health and Safety

One thing you should never do is take life for granted. Be thankful for what you have and don't be angry or resentful about what you don't have. Many people around the world are not as fortunate as you.

If you doubt this, take a walk through the floors of any Children's Hospital. You will see many smart, young teenagers who are just like you but are not healthy. They're not complaining about not getting an "A" in school or not scoring 20 points in a basketball game. You will see many teenagers whose biggest wish is to get better so they can enjoy life without sickness or pain.

73

Remember, as long as you have good health and safety you have everything. Nothing is more important. Not money, not cars, not fame. Without good health and safety, nothing else seems to matter. Here is a tip from Dr. Perry. He says, *"Good health is an opportunity to live life to its fullest. Invest in your health. Exercise regularly and drink at least 1/2 ounce of water per day. Eat a balanced diet and do not smoke. Most importantly, get rest. We need a restful sleep to rejuvenate our bodies."*

Be thankful for what you have!

> *"We never appreciate the value of water until the well runs dry."*
>
> **-Benjamin Franklin**

> *"Many of the things you can count, don't count. Many of the things you can't count, really count."*
>
> **-Albert Einstein**

Help Others

> *"What you remember, what you measure yourself by, what you cling to as you get older is what you have done as a family, what you have done for others, your own naked humanity."*
>
> **-former First Lady Barbara Bush**

I have a friend, Cynthia Cherbak. Recently she asked me if I would be interested in talking to a group of teenagers about the skills necessary for succeeding in the *Real World*. I love helping teenagers achieve success, so naturally, I accepted.

As we were driving to the talk, Cynthia said there was something that she didn't tell me about this group of teenagers. My first thought was that there would be hundreds of them, and she was worried that I may be a little nervous. However, it was not what I was expecting.

Cynthia was taking me to speak to teenagers in prison. That's right, prison! She began preparing me for what I was about to face. She said that I would be speaking to some of the most dangerous, messed-up kids in Southern California. Some were in for theft, arson, battery, and even murder. She said that I could tell who the murderers were, because they would be dressed in orange clothes.

Cynthia was also kind enough to mention that these teenagers were only permitted one hour of recreation per week, (this is not a misprint) and that I would be *stealing* their hour of free time. Didn't this just make me feel wonderful!

As the inmates came into the room, you could see that they really weren't interested in listening. Mid-way through the talk, some began heckling me while others simply weren't paying attention. I thought to myself, what a waste of time.

My talk was only 20 minutes, so they had 40 minutes of recreation to do what they wanted. (Thank God!) The only problem was that I wasn't permitted to leave until their full hour was up. So Cynthia and I remained in the room with the prisoners, anxiously watching the clock.

All of a sudden I noticed that one of the biggest, baddest looking teenagers I have ever seen in my life was walking toward us. He was about 6'5", weighed about 225 lb. and was dressed in orange, which told me he was in for murder. I became more and more nervous the closer he got.

Finally, he was no more than two feet away and I thought to myself that this guy was going to take a swing at me. But to my surprise he extended his hand and said,

"Your talk was great. I want you to know that I listened and I appreciate that you came here tonight. No one cares about us. It

meant a lot to me that you took the time to come here. Do you think you could come back again?"

I almost cried after hearing him say this. I realized that I had done the right thing by speaking to the inmates. I was able to help at least one person and that's all that mattered. As he requested, I went back many more times to do my talk.

That's what helping others is all about. Doing something out of the goodness of your heart for someone else. Putting their interests before your own. Most people don't. Wouldn't the world be a better place if more people simply helped others?

In 1996 **Marcus Camby** won the NCAA Collegiate Basketball Player of the Year award. He led his school, the University of Massachusetts, to the Final Four. He also was named as a first team All-American and would be one of the top players selected in the NBA draft.

However, all of his basketball success didn't seem to matter much mid-way through the season. During one of his games he was on the way back to the locker room when he collapsed and fell to the ground. In a frantic panic, Marcus was rushed to the hospital, where he remained for a few days of observation.

While in the hospital he heard there was a very sick teenager named Harry Tambolleo. Harry suffered from a serious illness.

Harry was getting worse and even told his family that things weren't looking good for him. When Marcus heard this, he took it upon himself to walk down to Harry's room for a visit, even though they didn't know each other. Immediately, Harry perked up with a smile and became more lively in the following days.

Unfortunately, Harry's disease eventually took his life. But his father said on national TV that Marcus Camby had added much happiness to Harry's final days on earth.

Marcus was a star basketball player with a busy life. Yet he realized that it was more important to bring a little sunshine into the life of a sick person. He didn't have to make the effort to visit Harry, a person who he had never met. But he did. And because he did, because he put someone else's interest before his own, he touched many people's lives. He touched my life and I have never met Marcus Camby.

> *"Our rewards in life will always be in exact proportion to the amount of consideration we show toward others."*
>
> **-Earl Nightingale**

No matter who we are or what our age, one thing everyone can do is to help others. It is the best feeling you can have when you know inside that you have made a difference in someone's life by helping them. That's what the world and our society should be about, helping others. Especially the less fortunate.

> *"Do all the good you can, by all the means you can."*
>
> **-John Wesley**

Not everyone can be a professional athlete, movie star, lawyer, doctor or the President of the United States. But you can be a good person.

Be nice and kind to others. Encourage people, rather than putting them down or laughing at them. Help someone to understand something if they are having trouble.

Listed on the next two pages is what I believe are the key points to becoming a better person. Please take the time to read these over and over again. It is even a good idea to write them in your own hand writing on a sheet of paper and hang the list where you will be forced to see it everyday. For example, place the list by the light switch in your bedroom or on the door of your school locker.

<u>Be a Good Person</u>

* Remember what's really important in life: good health & safety, and the people you love & care about.

* Thank your parents and those who have helped you in your life. Also, tell them that you love and care about them.

* Show respect, loyalty, and love by always being honest and true to your word.

* Show support by always being there for family and friends.

* Don't argue or cause resentment. Life is too short!

* Listen when your friends and family need to talk.

*   Go out of your way to help others.

*   Make people smile and laugh.

*   Encourage and help children and elderly people. They need it more than anyone.

*   Keep your word and your promise.

*   Take responsibility for yourself and your actions.

*   Treat others as you would like to be treated.

*   Give respect to get respect.

*   Apologize with sincerity if you are wrong.

*   Always be honest, loyal and love your spouse or mate.

*   Tell those you really love and care about that you do. Then tell them again.

"You have to look in the mirror when you awake in the morning and before you go to bed at night. And the mirror doesn't lie about what it sees!"

-Unknown

One Last Message to You!

The principles you have just read are simple but they work. The choice is yours as to whether you will apply them to your everyday life. Whether you succeed or not in life is up to you. No one can do it for you. Not your parents, brothers and sisters, friends, teachers or anyone else. You have to decide within yourself.

No one can guarantee or promise what level of success you will achieve in your life. However, if you put these principles to work through daily practice, then YOU WILL begin to achieve success.

Remember:

> *"YOU START TODAY TO BECOME WHAT YOU WILL BE TOMORROW!"*
>
> *YOU CAN DO IT - THE TIME TO START IS NOW!!*

The_____
(Write Your Name Here)

SUCCESS PLANNER

_____
(Date)

Chapter 1:   It All Starts With a Dream

List five of your dreams. Don't be afraid to dream "big."

1._____

2._____

3._____

4._____

5._____

Failure Is Good

List three things you have failed at.

1._____

2._____

3._____

What I have learned from my three failures.

1._____

2._____

3._____

Chapter 2:   Turn Your Dreams into Goals

List three goals you WILL accomplish within each time period.

(One Year Goals)

1._____

2._____

3._____

(Three Year Goals)

1._____

2._____

3._____

(Five Year Goals)

1._____

2._____

3._____

_____   _____
(Your Signature)   (Date)

This is your contract with yourself!

Chapter 3:   Do You Have an Address Book?

List five friends you will stay in touch with FOREVER.

1._____

2._____

3._____

4._____

5._____

List three ways you will stay in touch with them.

1._____

2._____

3._____

Chapter 4: Research Careers - NOW!

List three careers that interest you.

1._____

2._____

3._____

Who do you know who works in these careers?

1._____

2._____

3._____

Call these people immediately and set an appointment to visit with them. In your meeting ask questions to learn more about their careers. Also, ask if you can intern for them.

Chapter 5: The Truth About Success and $

Success is all about happiness. List three things that bring you happiness.

1._____

2._____

3._____

List three reasons why they bring you happiness.

1._____

2._____

3._____

List three people that have the kind of success that you desire.

1._____

2._____

3._____

List three people you admire and respect.

1._____

2._____

3._____

Take the time to visit with all the people you have listed. Talk to them about how they have achieved things in their life and how they have become the people they are today. Start a friendship with them and stay in touch. Their characteristics, principles and ideas will cause you to think of how you can improve yourself. Remember: *"Success Leaves Clues!"*

Chapter 6:   Never Stop Learning

Learn About Myself

1. **Which five things do I value most in my life?**_____

_____

2. **Which five goals are most important to me?**_____

_____

3. **Who are the five most important people in my life?**_____

_____

4. **What would I do if I won $1,000,000 today?**_____

_____

5. **What would I do if I only had 6 months to live?**_____

_____

6. **Which one thing would I try if I knew I could not fail?**_____

_____

7.   **Which one thing would I change about the world?**
_____

_____

Reading

List three books you WILL read this year that will improve your knowledge.

1._____

2._____

3._____

Listening

List three teachers or counselors that you have learned the most from.

1._____

2._____

3._____

List one thing you have learned from each person that has made an impact on your life.

1._____

2._____

3._____

Chapter 7:   Always Believe in Yourself

Train Your Mind

List three reasons you WILL achieve each of your dreams.

1._____

2._____

3._____

Positive Attitude

List three ways you can show that you have a positive attitude.

1._____

2._____

3._____

Chapter 8:   Get Up When Life Knocks You Down

List three things you have tried that were difficult to achieve.

1._____

2._____

3._____

Why were they difficult to achieve?

1._____

2._____

3._____

Now that you know why they were difficult to achieve, what must you do to make achieving success easier?

1._____

2._____

3._____

Chapter 9:   Hard Work Pays Off

List three things you could have worked harder at, but didn't.

1._____

2._____

3._____

What could have been the positive result of each if you would have worked harder.

1._____

2._____

3._____

Chapter 10: Make the Right Choices

List three *wrong* decisions you have made.

1._____

2._____

3._____

What were the negative consequences from your decisions?

1._____

2._____

3._____

List three *right* decisions you have made.

1._____

2._____

3._____

What were the positive results from your decisions?

1._____

2._____

3._____

Do you see the difference? Think before making decisions!

Chapter 11:   Be Thankful for What You Have

List three things you are thankful for.

1._____

2._____

3._____

List three things your parents or loved ones have done for you out of love for you.

1._____

2._____

3._____

Tell them THANK YOU and that you appreciate it!

Chapter 12:   Help Others

List three ways you have helped people in the past.

1._____

2._____

3._____

List three ways you can consistently help people in the future.

1._____

2._____

3._____

List three characteristics that make you a good person.

1._____

2._____

3._____

Anyone CAN Be a Good Person All of the Time!

Read your *Success Planner* on a regular basis. This is your road map to success. You can achieve anything that you desire. Remember:

"IF YOU CAN DREAM IT, YOU CAN DO IT!"

"Teenagers Tips for Success!"

Students Will Learn:

* The essential HABITS for creating SUCCESS
* Why NOW is the time to PLAN your future
* Why NETWORKING is very important to SUCCESS
* How to set and achieve GOALS, and MUCH MORE!!!
* FREE Success Planner included!

Make check or money order payable to:
Positive Publishing
P.O. Box 532 / Montrose, CA 91021-0532

Schools or anyone ordering large quantities, please call 1-800-692-1103

Title	Copies	Price	Total
Teenagers Tips for Success!	_____	$11.95	_____
Shipping/Handling ($3.00 for 1-2 Bks / $3.50 for 3-4 Bks)			_____
CA Residents Add 8.25% Sales Tax			_____
		Total	_____

Speaking Engagements

James Malinchak is available for speaking engagements at any conference or school. For more information, please contact:

James Malinchak
James Malinchak International
P.O. Box 3944
Beverly Hills, CA 90212-0944

1-888-793-1196
Email: JamesMal@aol.com
website: http://www.Malinchak.com

Write to James Malinchak

I hope this book has changed your life! I would like to hear from you. Please write to me, explaining how this book has touched your life. Send letters or emails to:

James Malinchak International
P.O. Box 3944
Beverly Hills, CA 90212-0944

Email: JamesMal@aol.com
website: http://www.Malinchak.com